# WHAT IT MEANS TO BE A

# Mom

## A CELEBRATION OF THE HUMOR, HEART (AND CHAOS) OF MOTHERHOOD

JEWEL NUNEZ

Creator of *One Funny Mummy*

ADAMS MEDIA

NEW YORK   LONDON   TORONTO   SYDNEY   NEW DELHI

Adams Media
An Imprint of Simon & Schuster, Inc.
57 Littlefield Street
Avon, Massachusetts 02322

First Adams Media hardcover edition April 2021

ADAMS MEDIA and colophon are trademarks of Simon & Schuster.

For information about special discounts for bulk purchases, please contact Simon & Schuster Special Sales at 1-866-506-1949 or business@simonandschuster.com.

The Simon & Schuster Speakers Bureau can bring authors to your live event. For more information or to book an event contact the Simon & Schuster Speakers Bureau at 1-866-248-3049 or visit our website at www.simonspeakers.com.

Interior design by Colleen Cunningham, Erin Alexander, Stephanie Hannus, Alaya Howard, Julia Jacintho, Sylvia McArdle, Victor Watch, Priscilla Yuen
Interior images © Getty Images; 123RF

Manufactured in China

10  9  8  7  6  5  4  3  2  1

Library of Congress Cataloging-in-Publication Data
Names: Nunez, Jewel, author.
Title: What it means to be a mom / Jewel Nunez, creator of One Funny Mummy.
Description: First Adams Media hardcover edition. | Avon, Massachusetts: Adams Media, 2021. | Series: What it means.
Identifiers: LCCN 2020034997 | ISBN 9781507214558 (hc) | ISBN 9781507214565 (ebook)
Subjects: LCSH: Mothers--Humor. | Motherhood--Humor.
Classification: LCC PN6231.M68 N86 2021 | DDC 818/.602--dc23
LC record available at https://lccn.loc.gov/2020034997

ISBN 978-1-5072-1455-8
ISBN 978-1-5072-1456-5 (ebook)

For Everly and Sylvie

# Introduction

*Do you find yourself surviving on zero sleep,
endless coffee, and unlimited snuggles?*

*Do you wonder why your laundry mountain
never seems to shrink despite doing
countless loads around the clock?*

*Do you turn to your #momsquad for support, guidance,
and a good belly laugh…Every. Single. Day?*

If so, then welcome to motherhood!

Motherhood requires the patience of a saint, the perse-
verance of a toddler with a question, and the resource-
fulness of MacGyver with a paper clip. Despite what
many mom blogs might have you believe, motherhood
isn't all *Instagram*-worthy snacks, matching pajamas
for the whole family, and peaceful moments of siblings
playing together quietly. As much as we want to pretend
we have it all together, learning the art of winging it is

essential to navigating the epic journey from diapers to first steps and playdates to school days. Being a mom is an emotional roller coaster of doing your best to raise kind and decent human beings…and that's where *What It Means to Be a Mom* comes in!

Here you'll find more than 150 entries designed to lift you up when you've had a bad day, make you laugh out loud (or raise your coffee cup in solidarity), and inspire you to keep going no matter what—because it means everything to be a mom!

So if you're ready to feel seen *and* heard (not an easy task after kids!), turn these pages for some humor, encouragement, and good old-fashioned honesty. If you need a quick pick-me-up after a meltdown (your own or your child's), fill up your wine glass, grab some chocolate from your secret stash, and know that you're not alone. And if you're ready to celebrate everything that it takes to be a mom, dive into this book and enjoy!

Each day
BEGINS and ENDS
with L♥VE,
and SOMEWHERE in the
BIG FANTASTIC MESS
in the middle is
MOTHERHOOD.

**You know you're a mom when...** you find yourself **forgetting** your own name, **falling asleep** midsentence, uncontrollably **sighing**, **failing** to keep track of time, and **consuming** copious amounts of coffee.

Mom

# Motherhood is a journey,

except it's just traveling from room
to room putting away the
same toys all day long.

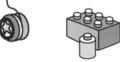

**IF you're lucky,** YOU FIND A MOM FRIEND YOU CAN TELL YOUR **Less-than-perfect** MOM MOMENTS TO, KNOWING SHE'D NEVER **judge** because she's been there herself.

One of the
**BEST PARTS** of
**MOTHERHOOD**
is when your kids make you
**FORGET YOU'RE A MOM**
and remind you what
it's like to

You know you're a mom when you have

EXCELLENT FLEXIBILITY

because you're always bending over backward for someone.

What's that thing called
when you never
sit down again?

# OH YEAH,
# MOTHERHOOD.

IF YOU'VE EVER SAID TO YOURSELF,

"I wish I could explain
every move I make
to someone all day long,"

THEN MOTHERHOOD IS FOR YOU.

Being a mom has its

**"I-CAN'T-DO-THIS-ANYMORE"**

moments, but it also has its

**"I'VE-NEVER-BEEN-HAPPIER-IN-MY-WHOLE-LIFE"**

moments that keep you going.

You know you're
a mom when...

SOMEONE TELLS YOU TO GO
TO YOUR HAPPY PLACE,
AND YOU GO BACK TO BED.

# MOTHERHOOD

took my SANITY away

but replaced it with

the craziest kind of

*love.*

IT'S EASY TO GO

# INCOGNITO

WHEN YOU'RE A MOM...
JUST WASH YOUR HAIR
AND PUT ON REAL PANTS.

# You know you're a mom when...

tick tick tick

9:15 IN THE MORNING SEEMS LATE IN THE DAY.

I want to say sorry to all the moms
I thought sounded mean before I had kids....

I TOTALLY
GET IT NOW.

You give your children the gift of life.

In return they give you the gift of learning what life is really about.

One day your **brain** works **fine**
and the **next** you're trying to **lock**
your **house** with your **car** remote.

# THANKS,

# MOTHERHOOD.

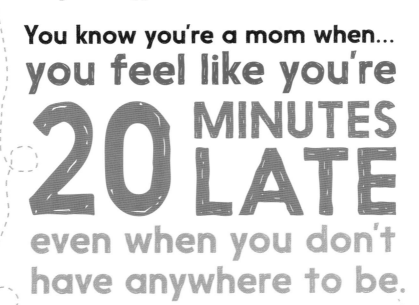

You know you're a mom when... you feel like you're **20** MINUTES LATE even when you don't have anywhere to be.

Motherhood brings out the best in you; it also brings out your gray hair and under-eye circles, but mostly your best.

DON'T BE
SO HARD
ON YOURSELF...
EVERY MOM IS
A WORK IN PROGRESS

## Mom Fact

### #127

Having kids makes you
appreciate and value
any "me time" you get,
even if it's just five minutes
before you pass out from
exhaustion at the
end of the day.

Even though your motherhood journey may change day to day, and sometimes hour to hour, the one unshakable constant is

**the love you have for your children.**

NOT UNTIL YOU
FULLY UNDERSTAND
THE SACRIFICES YOUR
OWN MOTHER MADE
WILL YOU TRULY KNOW
WHAT IT MEANS
TO BE A MOM.

Most of life with kids is trying to

 FAST-FORWARD

through the tough
moments while trying to

 PAUSE

the good ones.

I just laugh at the mom
I thought I was going to be—

THAT LADY HAD

NO IDEA

what she was in for.

# MOTHERHOOD IS...

sharing something from
your childhood that made
you happy and hoping
that it brings your kids
just as much joy.

**MOM MENTALITY:**

"I'll say yes to this one thing so they'll give me a break."

**KID MENTALITY:**

"Mom said yes, so let's ask her to do one hundred more things."

*Being a mom is a dream come true,* although sometimes it's like that dream where you're trying to run but you're stuck in slow motion.

# Which would you choose?

For your kids to sleep
past 7 a.m.

A laundry service
for a month

An ice-cream-of-
the-week subscription

The energy level of a
five-year-old

If you answered , then you're a part of the Mombies. Your ultimate dream is to be reacquainted with your long-lost friend, sleeping in. If you answered , then you're a part of the Maids of Motherhood. Your ultimate dream is to say goodbye to the shackles of your laundry and hello to freedom and fresh air. If you answered , then you're a part of the Nom Nom Moms. Your ultimate dream is to cozy up on the couch with just your spoon and the delicious flavor-of-the-week. If you answered , then you're a part of the Energizer Mommies. Your ultimate dream is to be able to get through your day without getting winded.

**SHOUT OUT** to *motherhood* **for making us** *experts on* **dealing with** *the unexpected.*

# MOTHERHOOD IS...

feeling like you're doing everything wrong and then being pleasantly surprised when your kids show you that you're actually doing something right.

OUR HOPES AND DREAMS CHANGE
ONCE WE BECOME MOMS. I USED TO
DREAM OF SUCCESS AND PROSPERITY,
BUT NOW ALL I HOPE FOR IS AN
UNINTERRUPTED
SHOWER.

The trick to motherhood is figuring out how to give all of yourself without *losing* all of yourself.

# MOMSPEAK DECODED

"I'll be right back."

↓

"Mommy needs a time-out."

"I'll think about it."

↓

"There's no way."

"Because I said so."

↓

"I can't think of a reason."

My parenting advice is simple:

LAUGH easily

Love intensely

NAP frequently

# M.O.M.s

**Makers of Memories**

**Managers of Madness**

**Marvels of Multitasking**

# Top Ten Inevitable Moments of Mom Life

10. Shoveling mac and cheese into your mouth over the stove.

9. Looking for your phone when it's in your hand.

8. Reheating your coffee until dinnertime.

7. Forgetting what you were saying midsentence.

6. Hiding in the bathroom to eat whatever treat you've stolen from your kids.

5. Unknowingly wearing your slippers to the grocery store.

4. Never knowing what day of the week it is.

3. Falling asleep while putting your kids to bed.

2. Having a "nice" pair of yoga pants you reserve for special occasions.

1. Hearing your mother's sayings coming out of your mouth.

Life as a mom is mostly
just wiping things
and making sure you have
enough things to wipe with.

When you become a mom,
you learn to be okay with doing all
the things your kids want to do

while squeezing what you
want to do into the last
thirty minutes of your day.

# MOM MATH

Take the age of your kids ___

x 2 ___

+ 10 months ___

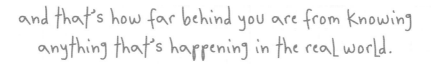

and that's how far behind you are from knowing
anything that's happening in the real world.

Being *proud* of your children
is an amazing feeling,
but having your children
be *proud* of you
is even better.

Sometimes all a mom longs to hear are those *three little words*: Time for bed.

# ABSENCE

MAKES THE HEART GROW FONDER
AND MUST BE WHY MOMS ARE
EXTREMELY FOND OF
**SLEEP** AND **SILENCE.**

# Mom Pie Chart

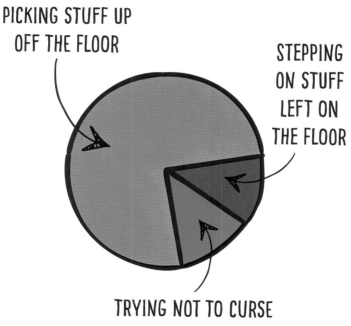

PICKING STUFF UP
OFF THE FLOOR

STEPPING
ON STUFF
LEFT ON
THE FLOOR

TRYING NOT TO CURSE
AFTER STEPPING ON
STUFF LEFT ON THE FLOOR

None of us know
exactly what
*motherhood*
has in store for us,
except for one guarantee:

*We'll know
unconditional love.*

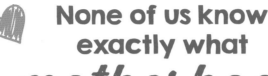

There will come a
time when you get frustrated
with motherhood, but that
doesn't make you a bad mom,
*that makes you normal.*

If you want to feel every emotion within the first five minutes of waking up each day, then motherhood is for you.

# Kids:

Shelter them, but not too much.

Protect them, but let them stumble.

Teach them, but let them discover.

Love them, no matter what.

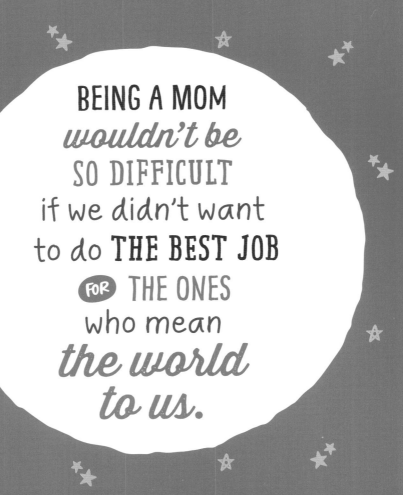

BEING A MOM
*wouldn't be*
SO DIFFICULT
if we didn't want
to do **THE BEST JOB**
**FOR** THE ONES
who mean
*the world*
*to us.*

# MOTHERHOOD IS...

being simultaneously
charmed and infuriated
by an adorable little
version of yourself.

When you sign up for
motherhood,
what you're really signing up for is
~~~ Loving ~~~
wholeheartedly
no matter the ups and downs
you encounter along the way.

**Me:**

The days are so incredibly long!

**Also me:**

The last five years have flown by!

MOTHERHOOD IS SO
SURPRISING; FOR INSTANCE,
YOU NEVER THOUGHT YOU'D
HAVE TO FORCE YOURSELF

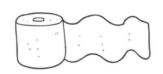

TO GO TO THE BATHROOM
FASTER BECAUSE A KID IS
SCREAMING AT YOU FROM
THE NEXT ROOM.

# Momboss

\mam'bos, məm'bos\ n

A mom who knows no sick days,

works overtime without pay,

and gives 110% of herself to her family.

# MOM'S LAUNDRY ADVISORY SYSTEM

1. SEVERELY STINKY
2. HIGHLY ODORIFEROUS
3. ELEVATED STENCH
4. MODERATE AROMA
5. LOW FUMES

# Mom Tip

GIVE NEW MOMS A BLENDER
AT THEIR BABY SHOWER.

IT DROWNS OUT THE CRYING
AND MAKES MARGARITAS.

WIN-WIN!

# AS A MOM

you get paid in hugs and kisses from the <u>best</u> bosses in the world, make your <u>own</u> schedule, and get to declare a national holiday <u>whenever</u> you choose.

# DESCRIBING

## MOTHERHOOD

is like playing Mad Libs but
the only words you can use

are _sticky_, _smelly_,
_(ADJECTIVE)_  _(ADJECTIVE)_

and _sleepy_.
_(ADJECTIVE)_

The reason why moms go over-the-top with birthday celebrations and gifts for their kids is because we're trying to say thank you for giving us the best gift in the world—motherhood.

REMEMBER to speak to *yourself* THE WAY YOU'D speak to your *children.*

# You know you're a mom when...

YOU'VE GONE FROM BEING SOMEWHAT COOL TO HAVING A PAIR OF EMERGENCY TWEEZERS FOR CHIN HAIRS IN YOUR PURSE AND A BOX OF TISSUES IN YOUR CAR.

*Every mom*
exists somewhere between
BEING HALF-
ASLEEP
and FEELING
HALF-
HUMAN.

I WAS GOING TO BE THAT MOM WHO NEVER GAVE HER KIDS CANDY UNTIL I REMEMBERED I LIKE THE SOUND OF SILENCE.

# MOTHERHOOD IS...

this amazing place
where what breaks you
fixes you just as easily.

A lot of what it takes to be a MOM is being a GOOD LISTENER, whether it's listening to your child's FEELINGS and CONCERNS, your friend's familiar STRUGGLES, or your own motherly INSTINCTS.

IF CLEANING UP ONE ROOM
WHILE EVERY OTHER ROOM
IN YOUR HOUSE IS
DESTROYED SOUNDS FUN, THEN
*you're going to
love motherhood!*

**Before motherhood:**

Hopes and dreams are ideas you nurture.

**After motherhood:**

Hopes and dreams become something you can hold in your arms.

You're never just a mom.

You are your child's everything.

# MOM BILL OF RIGHTS

ARTICLE 1: Freedom of because I said sos

ARTICLE 2: Freedom to wear yoga pants

ARTICLE 3: No Mom shall be quartered in any house with her children for longer than eight hours without reprieve

ARTICLE 4: No Mom shall be searched for treats not belonging to her or judged on the size of her wine pour

ARTICLE 5: Freedom of mind your own business

ARTICLE 6: No Mom shall be denied "me time" for more than two days in a row

ARTICLE 7: Freedom to scream into pillows

ARTICLE 8: No cruel and unusual punishments like questions before coffee

ARTICLE 9: No denying or disparaging Mom's cooking

ARTICLE 10: Freedom of Mom knows best

As moms we know it will all go too quickly,
so even though most days are exactly alike,
EMBRACE THE PREDICTABILITY
because that's what we're going to
look back on and miss the most.

## Mom Tip

ALWAYS REMEMBER THAT
LESS IS MORE WHEN FILLING OUT
A CARD FOR A NEW MOM AT
HER BABY SHOWER.

MORE IMPORTANTLY,
REMEMBER THERE IS SUCH A THING
AS BEING TOO HONEST.

The mom struggle
is real because
we fear we'll get it wrong
while trying our best
to get it right.

There are a lot of **big feelings** in motherhood, but the **biggest and best feeling** is sharing unbridled laughter with your children.

# MOTHERHOOD IS...

A RIDDLE OF OXYMORONS,
WRAPPED IN A STICKY MYSTERY,
INSIDE AN UNSOLVABLE ENIGMA
WHERE BRIBERY & GOLDFISH
CRACKERS ARE THE KEYS.

# MOTHERHOOD IS...

working as quickly as
possible to finish a
jigsaw puzzle only to get
to the last piece and
find it's missing.

WHEN YOU'RE BUSY WORRYING
ABOUT THE FUTURE, YOU'RE ACTUALLY
MISSING OUT ON THE PRESENT.

*Enjoy the*
*here and now*
*while it's still here.*

Being a mom is like
that scene in

*I Love Lucy*

with the conveyor belt,
except instead of chocolates,
it's dirty dishes making
their way to the sink.

&bull; MOM FRIENDS &bull;
ARE NECESSARY TO
*surviving* AND *thriving*
IN MOTHERHOOD, WHETHER
YOU'RE LAUGHING UNTIL YOU
CRY TOGETHER OR CRYING
UNTIL YOU LAUGH TOGETHER.

One of the most unbelievable things about being a mom is how you are

## NEEDED

one minute and

## IGNORED

the next.

THERE'S A NAME FOR MOMS WHO
DON'T STAY AWAKE ALL NIGHT
OVERTHINKING EVERY LITTLE THING:

*Those moms are called*

# DADS.

A LOT OF

*motherhood*

IS TAKING THE TIME TO

instill traditions

THAT MEAN THE MOST TO YOU
SO YOUR KIDS WILL HAVE

*a Legacy of Love*

TO PASS ON THROUGH
THE YEARS.

# HAVING IT
# ALL TOGETHER AS
# A MOM MEANS

you've showered, you've finished
every piece of laundry in the house,
and you have enough frozen
pizzas to feed the entire
neighborhood.

It's easy to feel like you're on your own in motherhood even when there's literally a child attached to your body twenty hours out of the day; but as moms, we share this common bond of wanting the best for our children, and that alone unites us all.

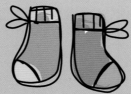

Diamonds might be a **girl's best friend,** but earplugs, *Netflix,* and black leggings are a **mommy's BFFs.**

*One of the best things about being a mom is that* even after you've had a bad day, you get the chance to start over *in the morning* or even *in the moment.*

By being forgiving of yourself, you teach your kids the same important lesson.

Motherhood
has its challenges—
like when you question
every decision you make—
but it also helps you find bravery
and strength to face those
tough moments like a

 MOMBOSS

Being a mom requires you to be a

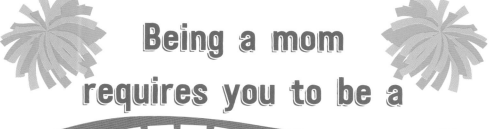

CHEERLEADER

for your kids when you feel

*anything but cheery.*

The sooner you learn that there's **NO** such thing as **PERFECTION** in motherhood, the sooner you get to truly **ENJOY** the **IMPERFECT MOMENTS** of life.

If you want perspective, have a baby, and then try to remember how easy it was to only take care of yourself.

The best mom friends
are the ones who
LISTEN TO YOU VENT,
WHO OFFER UNDERSTANDING
WITH JUST ONE LOOK,
AND WHO LET YOU KNOW
THEY SEE YOU
when it seems like
no one else does.

If you're not wishing for sleep when you blow your birthday candles out,

ARE YOU REALLY EVEN A MOM?

EVEN THOUGH OUR CHILDREN
FILL UP OUR LAUNDRY BASKETS
AND OUR KITCHEN SINKS,
THEY ALSO FILL OUR HEARTS
TO THE VERY BRIM.

THERE'S NO GUILT
LIKE MOM GUILT,

∽ BUT ∽

there's also no
stronger pride than

MOM PRIDE.

WE ALL WANT WHAT ANY MOM WANTS FOR HER KIDS; THAT THEY GROW UP TO BE HAPPY AND THAT THEY WIELD THEIR SARCASM FOR GOOD, NOT EVIL.

# A MOTHER'S WORK IS NEVER DONE

is the most accurate statement in the history of statements.

YOU'VE FOUND YOUR

# MOM TRIBE

— WHEN YOU —

SUPPORT, ENCOURAGE, AND
BUILD EACH OTHER UP,
REALIZING THAT MOTHERHOOD
IS HARD ENOUGH
WITHOUT BEING JUDGED AND SHAMED
FOR EVERY DECISION YOU MAKE.

# Mom Tip

DON'T FORGET TO JUMP OUT
FROM BEHIND THE CAMERA TO
GET IN THE PICTURE WITH YOUR KIDS
EVEN IF YOU'RE NOT "CAMERA-READY."

THESE SPONTANEOUS MOMENTS OF
REAL LIFE WILL END UP BEING
YOUR MOST CHERISHED PHOTOS.

# MOTHERHOOD IS...

needing to write
something down as soon
as it pops into your head,
but by the time you find
a pen or your phone,
it's gone.

One day you're a normal woman living in an ordinary world and then you *become* a *mom* and *life blossoms* in the most *extraordinary way.*

The comforting thing
about motherhood
is that even if you can't laugh
through the tough times
in the moment,
just remind yourself
that one day you will.

Being a mom is funny.
You look forward to bedtime
because you need a break—
but then once your kids are
in bed, all you do is look
at photos of them.

# Life with kids

is like living in a snow globe where the snow is...?

**A.** LEGO pieces

**B.** Playdough

**C.** Spaghetti

**D.** All of the above

Our children have the ability to mend
any heartache or anxiety,
*whether it's by*
wrapping their arms around us for a hug,
placing their small hands in ours,
*or even just*
flashing us a sweet smile.

## Mom Fact
## #54

Playdates are amazing ways for kids to socialize, but we all know they were really invented so moms could have a grown-up conversation about something other than My Little Pony or Pokémon.

# MOTHERHOOD IS...

different for every mom, but what we all have in common is that we welcome the unexpected and face the unknown with open arms.

# *Jeopardy!* for Moms

PATIENCE,
NICE THINGS,
LONG-TERM
PLANS

WHAT ARE THINGS MOMS DON'T HAVE?

We're warned *from* the beginning that it all goes too quickly, so we prepare ourselves not to let it happen, but like everything in motherhood, it's out of our control.

Having a little version of yourself
seems like a great idea
until you remember
how awful you were to your own parents.

You know you're a mom when...
you learn to appreciate *the little things*—

a *little* sleep,
a *little* free time,
a *little* bit of sanity...

There's no better feeling than giving your children exactly what they need at the moment they need it, whether it's a comforting hug, a reassuring smile, or an encouraging note in their lunch box.

A *mother's love* MEANS NOT HAVING ALL THE ANSWERS RIGHT AWAY BUT

DOING EVERYTHING POSSIBLE TO FIGURE OUT ANY PROBLEM.

What takes a normal person *a few minutes* to finish takes a mom *a few days* because of the constant snack requests and demands for help from the bathroom.

Mom life is defined as finally getting a half hour to yourself but needing to use it to shave your legs.

Look at yourself through the eyes of
your child and you'll see what they see:

*A beautiful, strong,
confident woman*

who always shows up for her
kids when they need her.

There will be those who try to tell you how your **motherhood story** should be written, but there's only one author and it's *you!*

# I LOVE BEING A MOM

BECAUSE NOW I CAN BLAME
THE YOGURT ON MY SHIRT AND
THE PEANUT BUTTER IN MY HAIR
ON MY KIDS

# Which would you choose?

 **A**
A yoga retreat

**B**
A mani/pedi

 **C**
Dancing all night

**D**
Staying in and bingeing Netflix

If you answered **A**, you're part of the Mom Tribe, where peace, quiet, and serenity bond you.

If you answered **B**, you're part of the Mom Squad, where rejuvenation and self-care reign.

If you answered **C**, you're part of the Mom Crew, where letting loose is your freedom.

If you answered **D**, you're part of the Mom Team, where comfort and calm bring happiness.

Some days our kids
drive us crazy,
but we never put
them to bed without
telling them we
love them like crazy.

YOU KNOW YOU'RE A MOM WHEN...

# YOU THINK FOUR HOURS of UNINTERRUPTED SLEEP is a LUXURY.

**Having children gives purpose to our lives, but more importantly, it gives us the will to**

# NEVER
*give up.*

THERE'S A LOT OF STUFF
NOBODY TELLS YOU ABOUT
BEFORE YOU
BECOME A MOM,
like how the bathroom becomes
*your sanctuary*
& how anything that
requires jumping
MAKES YOU PEE YOUR PANTS.

You can have good
blood pressure or
you can take your kids
to the grocery store.

You cannot have both.

Sharing
your truth
about motherhood
isn't about getting others
to agree with you;
it's about reaching that
one mom who relates
and needs to hear
that she's
not alone.

# ALL THE THINGS YOU NEVER THOUGHT YOU'D SAY AS A MOM:

"Stop licking the window!"

"Don't wipe boogers on your sister!"

"Fine, wear your pajamas to school!"

"Finish your pancakes or no doughnuts!"

# Mom Tip

ALWAYS TAKE A PHOTO AFTER
CLEANING YOUR HOUSE.

THAT WAY, WHEN THE KIDS
INSTANTLY TRASH IT, YOU CAN REMIND
YOURSELF WHY YOU EVEN BOTHERED.

*The old saying is true that raising children takes a village...*

# AND IT HELPS IF IT'S ONE WITH MANY VINEYARDS.

AT SOME POINT,

# BEING A MOM

STARTS TO FEEL MORE LIKE

negotiating with darling terrorists

who never back down until

THEY GET THEIR WAY.

There's nothing
more important than
the bond between
mother and child.
We make each other
who we are and
would be lost
without
one another.

# The Evolution of Motherhood

I love it so much!

It's way harder than I imagined!

It's making my eye twitch!

I'd do it all again in a heartbeat!

Our job as moms
is to guide our children
to create their own paths
⸙ —— and also —— ⸙
be the compass that helps them
find their way back to us.

## WHAT I SAID

"No."

## WHAT THEY HEARD

"Ask fifty more times."

# Which came first?

or

THE **MOM**

THE **MESSY BUN?**

# Top Three Essential Mom Must-Haves:

1. A DOG THAT LOVES CRUMBS

2. A LIFETIME SUPPLY OF MAGIC ERASERS

3. NOISE-CANCELING HEADPHONES

Embrace the
# MESSINESS
because it's
not going anywhere
until the kids
go off to college.

# Mom Poll

Where do you do your best thinking?

☐ IN THE SHOWER.

☐ IN THE CAR.

☑ WHO HAS TIME TO THINK?

VOTE

Even when you wake up
looking like you were
run over by a bus,
your kids will look at you
with nothing but
love and admiration in
their eyes, and that is
what makes being
a mom worthwhile.

"Put your shoes on, please."

"Empty your toy box looking for your kazoo, then do cartwheels down the hall."

You never know how much
you can handle until
you become a mom,
and then you learn you can
handle just about anything!

# ACCORDING TO TODDLER LAW,
anything you say CAN AND WILL
be used against you

and repeated at the most inappropriate times.

While you're nurturing the hearts and minds of your children, make time to do the same for yourself so that you can show up each day giving them your all.

"All we want is

# YOUR
# UNDIVIDED
# ATTENTION

and bottomless
bowls of snacks.
That's it."
—Kids

Seeing yourself
in your children
is the most indescribable
feeling of joy
and must be what walking
on sunshine feels like.

# MOTHERHOOD IS...

doing a million
different things
for only seconds
at a time.

One of the hard parts of raising kids
isn't getting them to listen—
it's making them think
everything is _T H E I R_ idea.

TRY YOUR BEST!

ASK QUESTIONS!

Motherhood Mantras

YOU GOT THIS!

TRUST YOUR GUT!

LAUGH IT OFF!

There's a sisterhood among
moms because we're all
a part of this thing
that at times feels impossible
but with each other's
support and friendship
becomes way more manageable.

# You Might Be a Mom If You're

- ☑ Tired as a mother
- ☑ Strong as a mother
- ☑ Prepared as a mother
- ☑ Loving as a mother
- ☑ Patient as a mother

If my kids learn nothing else from me, I hope they learn to be **HONEST** without being HURTFUL.

AS MOMS, WE MIGHT BE
UP WITH THE BIRDS, BUT AT LEAST
WE GET TO SEE SOME SPECTACULAR
*sunrises.*

MOMS are TRIPLE THREATS, but instead of *singing*, *dancing*, and *acting*, our talents are **negotiating** with strong-willed kids, knowing where every single thing is in the house, and making five different meals from leftovers.

A SUCCESSFUL MOM
MAKES SURE HER KIDS KNOW THEY

DESERVE THE WORLD

but are not entitled to it.

You can't raise *kind* and *decent* human beings if you're not a *kind* and *decent* human being *yourself*.

**Being a mom** isn't so much about creating a carefree life for your kids *as it is about* showing them how to deal with things when they don't go as planned.

# Moms have two speeds:

**HURRY**

Hurrying to
get the kids
somewhere
on time.

**HURRY**

Hurrying to
get the kids
to bed so you
can finally
stop moving.

The hardest stage of motherhood is whatever one you're going through.

Want to laugh in the most surprising ways?

Have kids—they will keep you laughing
*until it hurts.*

Remember that you're allowed to leave the dishes until morning, especially when your kids ask you to cuddle on the couch.

All that sleep was **SUPER ANNOYING** anyway.

—Lies parents tell themselves

YOU SAY,
**MOM;**
I SAY,

HAPPINESS CURATOR.

# You know you're a mom when...

YOU WAKE UP EARLIER THAN
YOU HAVE TO JUST TO
ENJOY PEACE AND QUIET.

LEARNING
WHEN TO LET GO &
WHEN TO HOLD ON IS
A MOM'S MOST
VALUABLE SKILL.

A mother's love is measured in...

# HUGS, KISSES, & PANCAKES

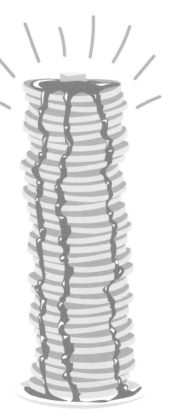

You know you're
a mom when...

SEEING YOUR CHILD'S FACE
INSTANTLY IMPROVES YOUR DAY.

"Could you repeat that?"

—Said no parent ever

When you have kids
your heart SWELLS and EXPANDS,
making your capacity

FOR LOVE
greater
THAN
EVER.

you know you're a mom when...
the title of your autobiography would be

I LOVE HOW MY KIDS ASK ME TO DO TWENTY THINGS AT ONCE LIKE I'M SOME KIND OF WIZARD.

I AM, BUT THEY DON'T NEED TO KNOW THAT.

WHEN YOU CULTIVATE
A LIFE WITH YOUR FAMILY
YOU'RE FOSTERING
THE GROWTH OF HAPPY,
HEALTHY CHILDREN,
AND THAT'S THE

*magic of
motherhood.*

YOU KNOW YOU'RE A MOM WHEN...
*your favorite moments*
are never the carefully
orchestrated ones,
BUT THE AUTHENTIC,
OUT-OF-THE-BLUE ONES
THAT MAKE YOU SMILE
WHENEVER YOU
remember them.

## Mom Fact #15

Mom life = best life

# BE THE MOM
*whom your children*
## ADMIRE,
## RESPECT,
**AND** ## ASPIRE
*to be like one day.*

IF YOU ASK A GROUP OF WOMEN WHAT IT *MEANS* TO BE A MOM, YOU'LL GET DIFFERENT ANSWERS, BUT AT THE CENTER OF THOSE ANSWERS YOU'LL FIND UNCONDITIONAL

*love,*

PATIENCE,

AND A SENSE OF

BECAUSE THAT'S WHAT IT *TAKES* TO BE A MOM.

Resilient moms RAISE resilient kids

Once upon a time...
I could complete a
thought, and then

I became a mom.

THE END.

If it doesn't challenge you,
it doesn't change you, so it's

**NO SURPRISE THAT**

motherhood has changed
every single thing
about me.

Sometimes you don't have the right words for your kids when you need them,

but you always have more than enough love to give them.

EVENTUALLY,
EVERY MOM REACHES THE
"IT'S-A-GOOD-THING-YOU'RE-SO-CUTE"
STAGE.

THERE'S NOTHING GREATER IN motherhood THAN HEARING YOUR CHILD SAY, "I ♥ you, Mom."

AS A MOM YOU GIVE UP SO MUCH,
BUT WHAT YOU GET BACK IN RETURN IS

*worth every*

SACRIFICE

*big* and *small.*

## MOM BLESSING

*May you have:*

**THE CREATIVITY**
*of Martha Stewart*

**THE PATIENCE**
*of Mother Teresa*

**THE KINDNESS**
*of Carol Brady*

**THE WISDOM**
*of Mary Poppins*

If you were indecisive
before becoming a mom,
then there's good news—
you'll now be forced into making

# a thousand
# small decisions
# a day.

# About the Author

Jewel Nunez is a humorist who started her blog, *One Funny Mummy*, when her daughter was just six months old as a way to help her figure out exactly what it meant to be a mom. Today, she has two little girls, not one shred of sanity left, and (still!) doesn't have this whole motherhood thing totally figured out. In her rare spare time, she enjoys family hikes, educating her children on the importance of '90s rap, and searching for the best hiding spot to drink her coffee while it's still hot. Learn more about her parenting adventures at OneFunnyMummy.com.